FEAST FOR 10

CATHRYN FALWELL

SCHOLASTIC INC.

New York   Toronto   London   Auckland   Sydney

Text and illustrations copyright © 1993 by Cathryn Falwell.
All rights reserved. Published by Scholastic Inc.,
555 Broadway, New York, NY 10012, by arrangement with
Houghton Mifflin Company.
Printed in the U.S.A.
ISBN 0-590-48466-4

8 9 10   14   01 00 99 98 97

For
my family

in
loving memory
of
my grandmothers

Willie Mae McMullen Chauvin
and
Evelyn Haning Falwell

who often made
feasts for plenty

4

1 one
cart
into the
grocery
store

2 two
pumpkins
for pie

3 three
chickens
to fry

 **four
children
off to
look for
more**

5 five kinds of beans

6 six
bunches
of greens

 seven
dill pickles
stuffed in
a jar

 eight
ripe
tomatoes

14

9 nine
plump
potatoes

10 ten
hands
help
to load
the car

16

Then . . .

1 one
car
home
from the
grocery
store

2 two
will
look

3 three
will
cook

4 four
will
taste
and ask
for
more

5 five
empty
cans

6 six
pots and
pans

7 seven
more carrots
to wash
and
peel

8 eight
platters
down

9 nine
chairs
around